# Contents

Some words in this book appear in **bold**, like this. You can find out what they mean by looking in the glossary

# What is a microhabitat?

A **habitat** is a place where an animal lives. Habitats include deserts, rainforests, rivers, oceans and meadows. A **microhabitat** is a smaller area where animals live. There are many microhabitats within a habitat.

# Microhabitats

## At Home with the Minibeasts

Claire Throp

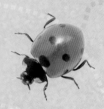

Raintree is an imprint of Capstone Global Library Limited, a company incorporated in England and Wales having its registered office at 264 Banbury Road, Oxford, OX2 7DY – Registered company number: 6695582
www.raintree.co.uk
myorders@raintree.co.uk

Edited by Helen Cox Cannons
Designed by Cynthia Della-Rovere
Original illustrations © Capstone Global Library Limited 2018
Picture research by Tracy Cummins and Heather Mauldin
Production by Tori Abraham
Originated by Capstone Global Library Limited
Printed and bound in India

ISBN 978 1 4747 6629 6 (hardback)
22 21 20 19 18
10 9 8 7 6 5 4 3 2 1

ISBN 978 1 4747 6630 2 (paperback)
23 22 21 20 19
10 9 8 7 6 5 4 3 2 1

**British Library Cataloguing in Publication Data**
A full catalogue record for this book is available from the British Library.

**Acknowledgements**
We would like to thank the following for permission to reproduce photographs: Alamy: Biosphoto/Quentin Martinez, 4, Matthias Lenke, 25, 29 Top Middle, Richard Becker, 11, Robert Pickett, 18, 28 Bottom Left; iStockphoto: athinaenglandphotography, 12, Chris Mansfield, 7, Henrik_L, 17, 29 Top Right, SemenovIgor, 15; Shutterstock: Alena Popova, 16-17 Background, Alex Staroseltsev, 1 Top Right, 31, Allexxandar, 24-25 Background, Astrid Gast, 27, 29 Bottom Right, azure1, 10 Background, Barbro Bergfeldt, 18-19 Background, chanwangrong, 26 Background, Daniel_Kay, 4-5 Background, David Dohnal, 21, Dlabajdesign, 22, Erni, 28 Top Right, Grimplet, 3 Top, Ian Grainger, 8, Ian Rentoul, 28 Top Left, ifong, 12-13 Background, irin-k, Cover Top, Back Cover, 1 Top Left, 1 Bottom, 3 Bottom, 32, Keattikorn, Design Element, kenjii, 6-7 Background, Kiolk, 24, 29 Bottom Middle, Madlen, 14-15 Bottom, Manfred Ruckszio, 26, Marcel Jancovic, 13, Marek R. Swadzba, 20, Maryna Pleshkun, 29 Top Left, Matt Hudson, 16, 29 Bottom Left, mikroman6, 6, NataliTerr, 11 Background, Nutnarin Khetwong, 20-21 Background, PHOTO FUN, 19, SADLERC1, 23, schankz, Cover Bottom, Seksan44, 5, SIMON SHIM, 9, thatmacroguy, 10, windu, 14-15 Background Yulia Kupeli, 8-9 Background, zhekoss, 22-23 Background, 28 Bottom Right

Every effort has been made to contact copyright holders of material reproduced in this book. Any omissions will be rectified in subsequent printings if notice is given to the publisher.

stag beetle

This book looks at habitats you can find in your local area. These include gardens and parks. Microhabitats within these habitats include holes in walls, plants, piles of rotting leaves and spaces under rocks or plant pots. Minibeasts live in these microhabitats. Larger animals often pass by microhabitats looking for something to eat ... like minibeasts!

# What lives on plants and flowers?

Plants and flowers are **microhabitats**. They are homes to many minibeasts. Minibeasts can find **shelter** under leaves and food from flowers. Bees and butterflies help to spread **pollen** to make new flowers.

**Ladybird**
Length: up to 10 millimetres
Eats: aphids, small insects
What eats it: some birds and spiders
How long it lives for: 2–3 years

## Aphids and ladybirds

Aphids live and feed on plants. Ladybirds love to eat aphids. The bright colour of ladybirds shows that they are **poisonous** to **predators**. But some birds and spiders can eat the ladybirds.

**Aphid**

Length: 1–7 millimetres

Eats: plant **sap**

What eats it: ladybirds, some wasps, insect **larvae**

How long it lives for: between 7 and 40 days

## Froghoppers

Froghoppers live on plants. They are tiny **insects** that can jump up to 70 centimetres in the air! Their young, called nymphs, are covered in froth. The froth is also known as "cuckoo spit". The nymphs live on plant stems. Froth protects the nymphs from **predators**. The nymphs make the froth themselves. They push air into liquid that comes out of their bottoms.

cuckoo spit

## Froghopper

**Length**: about 6 millimetres

**Eats**: adults eat plant **sap**; nymphs eat young leaves

**What eats it**: small birds

**How long it lives for**: 23 days (adult)

## Leaf-cutter bees

Leaf-cutter bees live in holes in plant stems, dead wood or old walls. The females cut discs out of leaves. You may have seen bees carrying bits of leaves in your garden. The bees glue the discs together with saliva. Saliva is a liquid found in their mouths. They use the discs to make "rooms" in which their **larvae** live.

### Leaf-cutter bee

**Length**: 1.3 centimetres
**Eats**: pollen, nectar
**What eats it**: some species of wasps feed on their larvae
**How long it lives for**: 3–4 months (females)

adult cranefly

# What lives in soil?

Some minibeasts live in soil.

### Leatherjackets
Young cranefly are known as leatherjackets. They live underground and feed on grass roots. Adult cranefly are often known as daddy-long-legs.

## Earthworms

Earthworms usually live in the top few centimetres of soil. They help to keep the soil healthy. The hairs on their body allow them to grip the earth and move through the soil. You can find earthworms in your garden or nearby park.

### Earthworm

**Length**: up to 30 centimetres

**Eats**: rotting roots and leaves, and remains of dead animals

**What eats it**: birds, shrews, mice, frogs, lizards, beetles, slugs

**How long it lives for**: 4–8 years

# What lives in a compost heap?

A compost heap contains rotting leaves, vegetables and other waste. Many minibeasts live and feed there. They attract **predators** such as hedgehogs and blackbirds. The predators feed on the minibeasts.

## Earwigs

Earwigs live in compost heaps as well as under plant pots or rocks. They have wings but rarely fly. Females lay 20–30 eggs. Unlike many **insects**, they look after their young when the eggs hatch.

### Earwig

**Length**: up to 15 millimetres

**Eats**: plant matter, flowers, small insects, aphids

**What eats it**: toads, birds, beetles

**How long it lives for**: 1–3 years

# Harvestmen

A harvestman lives in damp places in your garden. It is not a spider. It cannot make webs. Instead, the harvestman uses hooks on the ends of its legs to capture **prey**. If caught itself, it gives off a horrible smelling liquid.

### Harvestman
**Length**: up to 30 millimetres across
**Eats**: small insects, worms, snails
**What eats it**: birds, toads, spiders, wasps
**How long it lives for**: 1 year

## Woodlice

Woodlice live in compost heaps or under bark or plant pots in your garden. Pill woodlice are able to curl up in a ball to protect themselves from **predators**. Some woodlice climb trees to find **algae** to eat!

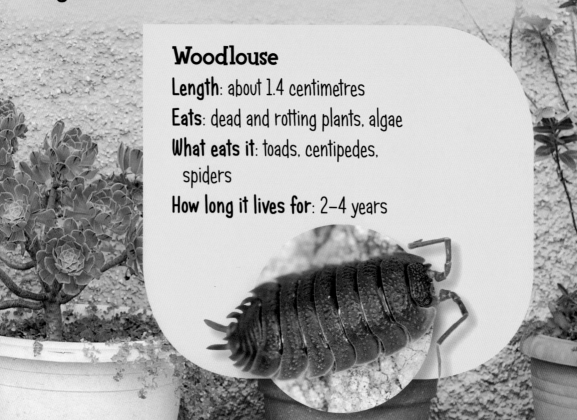

### Woodlouse

**Length**: about 1.4 centimetres
**Eats**: dead and rotting plants, algae
**What eats it**: toads, centipedes, spiders
**How long it lives for**: 2–4 years

## Flat-backed millipedes

The flat-backed millipede lives in compost heaps and other dark, damp places in your garden. It has many sections to its body. These are called segments. It has two pairs of legs on each segment. Millipedes can have from 40 to 400 legs!

### Flat-backed millipede

**Length**: 2.4 centimetres
**Eats**: dead and rotting plants, mildew
**What eats it**: birds, shrews, badgers
**How long it lives for**: 2–3 years

The pill millipede looks a lot like the pill woodlouse. The only way to tell them apart is by the number of legs. The pill millipede has only 18 pairs of legs but this is more than the pill woodlouse, which has just 7 pairs.

pill millipede

Buzzing snail hunter

# What lives in leaf litter and logs?

Some minibeasts live in piles of rotting leaves called leaf litter. Others live in dead logs. Have a look for them in woods or parks near where you live.

## Buzzing snail hunters

The buzzing snail hunter is a beetle. It lives under logs. It buzzes like a wasp if you pick it up. This beetle has a long "snout" that allows it to eat snails.

**Common centipede**

**Length**: about 3 centimetres

**Eats**: small **insects**, earthworms, slugs, spiders

**What eats it**: birds, toads, shrews, mice

**How long it lives for**: 5–6 years

## Common centipedes

Common centipedes live under rocks, logs and plant pots. Their bodies are made up of parts called segments. Each segment has one pair of legs. They have 15 pairs of legs altogether. They can crawl backwards as well as forwards.

## Great grey slug

The great grey slug is also known as the leopard slug. It has spots like a leopard. It lives in leaf litter and in damp places like old logs. You may have seen them feeding on plants in your garden!

## Garden snails

Garden snails feed at night. They spend the day in **sheltered** places such as underneath stones or in gaps in trees. If it is too dry, they seal themselves into their shells. They can live like that for months.

### Great grey slug
**Length**: up to 20 centimetres
**Eats**: plants; other slugs
**What eats it**: birds, shrews, toads
**How long it lives for**: up to 3 years

22

Garden snail

# What lives in ponds?

Ponds are home to many different minibeasts. Larger animals such as frogs live there too. Frogs eat minibeasts. If you have a pond in your garden or in your area, try to look for minibeasts in there. Be careful not to fall in!

## Pond skaters

Pond skaters are **insects** that live around small ponds or ditches. They can run fast across the water. They use their front legs to snatch up insects that have landed on the water's surface.

### Pond skater

**Length**: 15 millimetres
**Eats**: small insects
**What eats it**: frogs, toads, fish, birds
**How long it lives for**: 1–6 months

### Whirligig beetles

Whirligig beetles live in ponds and ditches. They spin round on the surface of the water as they look for food. They have one pair of eyes, but each eye is divided into two parts. This is so they can see above and below water at the same time.

## Giant house spider

**Length of body:**
1.4–1.6 centimetres

**Leg span:** up to 7.5 centimetres

**Eats:** flies, **insects**, moths

**What eats it:** cellar spider

**How long it lives for:**
about 3 years

## Peacock butterfly

**Wing span:** 63–69 millimetres

**Eats:** nectar; nettles
(caterpillar)

**What eats it:** birds (caterpillar),
spiders

**How long it lives for:**
11 months

# What lives in sheds and houses?

Some minibeasts live indoors. Spiders live in sheds, garages and houses.

### Giant house spiders

A male giant house spider searches for a female in the autumn. They **mate** and then the female eats the male!

### Peacock butterflies

In autumn, peacock butterflies drink a lot of **nectar** from flowers such as lavender. This helps them to survive the winter. They live in sheds and garages during those cold months.

# What is a food chain?

Food chains show
what animals eat.

Foxes eat shrews.

Shrews eat minibeasts
such as slugs, snails,
beetles, centipedes
and millipedes.

The minibeasts
eat leaf litter.

# Quiz

1. Which minibeast has eyes that are divided in two?

a) earthworm     b) whirligig beetle     c) woodlouse

2. How many pairs of legs does a pill millipede have?

    a) 1,000                b) 7                c) 18

3. Which minibeast has hooks on the ends of its legs to help it catch its food?

a) harvestman     b) pond skater     c) peacock butterfly

# Glossary

**algae**  plant-like living things with no stems or leaves that grow in damp places

**habitat**  natural place in which a plant or animal lives

**insect**  animal with a hard outer shell, six legs, three body sections and two feelers; most insects have wings

**larvae**  insects at the stage of development between an egg and an adult

**mate**  come together to produce young

**microhabitat**  small part of a larger area, where minibeasts live

**nectar**  sweet liquid found in many flowers

**poisonous**  able to harm or kill with poison

**pollen**  powder made by flowers to help them create new seeds

**predator**  animal that hunts other animals for food

**prey**  animal hunted by another animal for food

**sap**  liquid found inside plants and trees

**shelter**  safe, covered place

# Find out more

## Books

*It's All About … Beastly Bugs* (Kingfisher, 2016)

*Minibeasts* (My First Book of Nature), Victoria Munson (Wayland, 2017)

*The Big Book of Bugs,* Yuval Zommer (Thames and Hudson, 2016)

## Websites

**www.buglife.org.uk/activities-for-you/children-and-schools/bug-buddies-activities-young-people**

Go to this website and download the Bug Buddies magazines to find out more about minibeasts.

**www.dkfindout.com/uk/animals-and-nature/earthworms-and-leeches/earthworms**

Learn more about worms on this website.

# Index

Answers to quiz on page 29
a) harvestman
b) whirligig beetle
c) 18